Contents

Words printed in bold **like this** are explained in the Glossary.

Pig relatives

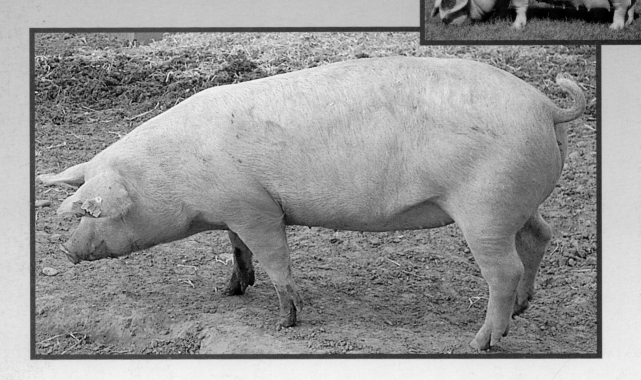

Most pig farmers keep large, pink pigs. These grow well and have lots of baby pigs. Pigs like the Gloucester Old Spot in the top picture do not grow quickly, but they look interesting.

Farm Animals

Pigs

This item is to be returned on or before the latest date above.

It may be borrowed for a further period if not in demand.

Warwickshire
County Council

Libraries · Heritage · Trading Standards

The author wishes to thank Michael and Angela, farmer Jamie and Cressida.

First published in Great Britain by Heinemann Library
Halley Court, Jordan Hill, Oxford OX2 8EJ,
a division of Reed Educational and Professional Publishing Ltd.
Heinemann is a registered trademark of Reed Educational & Professional Publishing Limited.

OXFORD MELBOURNE AUCKLAND
JOHANNESBURG BLANTYRE GABORONE
IBADAN PORTSMOUTH NH (USA) CHICAGO

Designed by AMR
Originated by Ambassador Litho Ltd
Printed in Hong Kong/China

05 04 03 02 01
10 9 8 7 6 5 4 3 2 1

ISBN 0 431 10087 X
This title is also available in a hardback library edition (ISBN 0 431 10080 2)

British Library Cataloguing in Publication Data
Bell, Rachael, 1972–
  Pigs. – (Farm animals)
  1.Swine – Juvenile literature
  I.Title
  636.4

Acknowledgements
The Publishers would like to thank the following for permission to reproduce photographs:
Agripicture/Peter Dean pp 6; Farmers Weekly Picture Library, pp 8, 13, 18, 20; Garden Matters pp 12 & 16/John Phipps; Holt Studios pp 4 t, 14 & 28 b/Sarah Rowland, 4 b,10, 11, & 24/Nigel Cattlin, 25/Gordon Roberts; Chris Honeywell p 22, 27; Images of Nature/FLPA pp 5/Silvestris, 9/E & D Hosking, 15/J. C. Allen, 17/Peter Dean, 26/M. Nimmo; NHPA p 19/B. A. Janes; d. b. Pineider p 23; Lynn M Stone p 28 t; Tony Stone Images pp 7/H. Richard Johnston, 21/Andy Sacks.

Cover photograph reproduced with permission of Farmers Weekly Picture Library.

Our thanks to Tony Prior, Bowers Farm, Wantage, Oxon, for his comments in the preparation of this book.

Every effort has been made to contact copyright holders of any material reproduced in this book. Any omissions will be rectified in subsequent printings if notice is given to the Publisher.

For more information about Heinemann Library books, or to order, please phone 01865 888066, or send a fax to 01865 314091. You can visit our web site at www.heinemann.co.uk

Wild pigs are called wild **boar**. They live in some forests and can be fierce. They are smaller than farm pigs. Their coats are darker and more hairy.

Welcome to the pig farm

On this pig farm the farmer keeps pigs and a few cows. The only other animals on the farm are two pet dogs.

Although this is a pig farm, much of the land is used for growing **crops** like wheat or barley. Some of the wheat and barley is **milled** and fed to the pigs.

Meet the pigs

ears

tail

snout

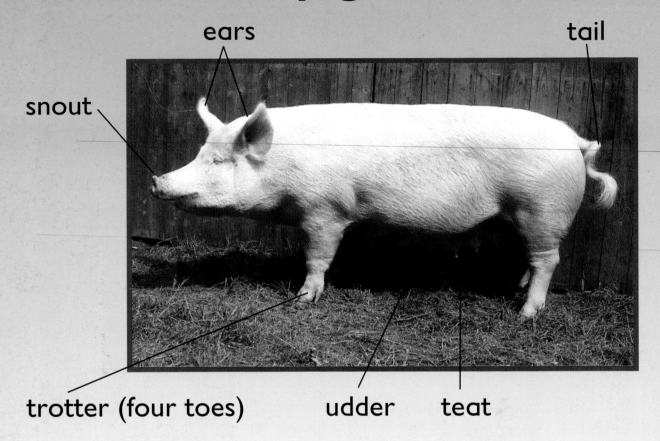

trotter (four toes)   udder   teat

Female pigs are called **sows**. They eat lots of food to make enough milk to feed their **piglets**. Some sows eat ten kilograms of food every day.

tusk

Male pigs are called **boars**. They are a bit taller than you, but weigh about ten times more! They eat less than sows, but they fight more, using their **tusks**.

Meet the baby pig

A baby pig is called a **piglet**. It can walk almost as soon as it is born. It weighs about one kilogram, the same as a bag of sugar.

Sows usually have about 11 piglets in each **litter**. The sow makes the piglets feed regularly. Every 20 minutes she grunts to call them to feed from her.

Where do pigs live?

On this farm the pigs live in indoor **pens**. They have **straw bedding** to keep them clean and warm. The farmer changes the straw every two days.

The pigs lie in one area that is warm and dry. They get up to eat in the other area. This has a feed **trough** and a **water drinker**.

What do pigs eat?

Pigs can bite, chew and drink, like us. They eat meat and plants. Most pig food is made from plants and is a bit like your breakfast cereal!

At three weeks old the **piglets** leave
their mother. They eat special **pellets**.
Older pigs eat liquid food, like thick
soup. This is easy to feed to lots of pigs.

How do pigs stay healthy?

Pigs play-fight almost as soon as they are born. This is good exercise and keeps them fit. It also helps them find out their **pecking order**.

Pigs like to **wallow** in wet mud or **straw**. This keeps them cool in hot weather. Some farms use water sprinklers to give them cold showers!

How do pigs sleep?

Pigs are most active at dawn, when the sun comes up, or at dusk, when it goes down. Between these times they sleep in nests made in their **straw**.

When a pig sleeps, it likes to lie on its side with its legs out straight. Pigs sleep close to each other to keep warm. They wake up a few times to eat and drink.

Who looks after the pigs?

On a large pig farm, several people look after the pigs. One person looks after the **sows** and **piglets**, and someone else looks after the older piglets.

This person is making sure the piglets are well. Sometimes the **vet** is called when the pigs are ill.

What are pigs kept for?

People keep pigs because we eat their meat, called pork. It is made into many different foods. Most sausages are made with **minced** pork. Bacon and ham are also made from pork.

In some countries, people use leather made from pigskin to make clothes and shoes. It feels very soft and smooth. Some brushes are made from pig **bristles**.

Other kinds of pig farm

On some pig farms the pigs spend
most of their time outdoors in a field.
Their food is scattered on the ground.
They go into their huts for shelter.

Other pig farms keep their pigs in large buildings. The pigs grow faster indoors, and do not need to put on fat to keep warm.

Organic pig farms

A few pig farms **rear** organic pigs.
This means the pigs do not usually eat
medicines in their food unless they
are ill. Most organic pigs live outside.

The meat from organic pigs costs more than ordinary pork. The pigs grow more slowly. Some people feel this pork tastes better.

Fact file

 If you grew as quickly as a newborn **piglet**, you would double your weight every week!

 Some **sows** have as many as 35 piglets in a year! Sows usually have 12 **teats**, so any more piglets have to be given to another sow to feed.

 Some **boars** weigh as much as a small car!

In the wild, pigs find food by rooting around the ground with their **snout** and eating whatever they find – acorns and other nuts. They have a very good sense of smell. In France and northern Italy farmers train their pigs to smell out truffles, special mushrooms that grow underground.

 Farmers used to say that the only thing you could not eat from a pig was its squeak! This is because people learned how to cook and use every part of the pig, even the **trotters.**

Glossary

bedding   what pigs lie on

boar   male or father pig. Also the name for a wild pig.

bristles   the whiskers and short, stiff hairs

crops   plants farmers grow in their fields

female   the girl or mother

joints   legs or shoulders of an animal

litter   group of animals born together from one mother

male   the boy or father

medicine   liquid or tablet taken when you are ill, often given to animals to make them grow faster

milled   ground up

minced   chopped up finely or put through a mincer

pecking order   pigs need to know which pig is more important than another, so that they know who is boss!

pellets   dry pig food that has been mixed and then pressed into tiny pieces

pens	name given to the rooms that pigs live in
piglets	baby pigs
rear	bring up young children or animals
sow	the female or mother pig
snout	the nose and mouth
straw	dried stalks from the wheat and barley crops
teats	the mouth pieces on the sow's milk bag that the piglets suck from
trotters	feet of a pig
trough	big food holder that the pigs eat from
tusks	the two large teeth that grow up out of the mouth of a boar
vet	a doctor for animals
wallow	pigs lie in cool mud to keep cool because they cannot sweat
water drinker	type of water fountain for pigs

More books to read

Story books
Pig in the Pond, Walker Books
3 Little Wolves and the Big Bad Pig! Walker Books
Honk! Honk! Walker Books
Pig Tale, Egmont

Information books
Animal Young – Mammals, Heinemann Library
Images – On the Farm, Heinemann Library
The Farming Year, Autumn, Winter, Spring, Summer,
  Wayland
Mealtimes – Evening Meals Around the World,
  Wayland

Index